Particular

I0117863

Peter Vealey

chipmunkapublishing

the mental health publisher

Peter Vealey

Published by

Chipmunkapublishing

PO Box 6872

Brentwood

Essex CM13 1ZT

United Kingdom

http://www.chipmunkapublishing.com

Chipmunkapublishing gratefully acknowledge the support of Arts Council England.

2

Author Biography

I am Peter Vealey,
Fifty Nine years in the making.
Born in Bishop`s Stortford, Herts.
This is my second collection of poems called "Particular".
My first was called "With Authentic Stains ", published in September 2008.
Within this book are varied poems over many years of my life.
From my teenage years to the present.
Unashamedly compassionate, politically thought-provoking and observational.

Peter Vealey

Preface

This is my second collection of poems, called "Particular".

This is a far wider range of poems and unashamedly "Particular", covering many subjects including my periods of working life, unemployment and social exclusion.
Also, poems about the changing political landscape in the U.K and the world.

From the more tolerant social climate of the sixties, to the present time. Other topics covered, include humanity, global environment, celebrity culture, materialism.

The book is called "Particular", because of my political and social leanings.

As with my first book it reiterates my strongly held passion for social justice
And democracy in the United Kingdom.

The home of the "Mother of Parliaments" and the wider world.

This book is dedicated to "Bubbles"-Dad.

Peter Vealey

Acknowledgements

Thanks to Peter at graphics54@yahoo.co.uk for his invaluable help with the cover illustration.

Also thanks to Rene Dixon and Dean Weston for their continued support, and encouragement with this body of work for my second book.

Peter Vealey

All the glossy panaceas

All the glossy panaceas,
Uttered from calm soothing politicians.
Of all the "preventative measures and unlikely worst-case scenarios.
You have to take into account".
Will not change human weakness,
Often in reality just selfish cruelty.
And the days are too long at "keep cool"
When there`s devil in the sheep.
For there`s a point,
Far beyond controlled exasperation.
When we all say.....!
And the death wish in us all
Is plainly there for us to see.
Likened to the brutal history of mankind.
Not a pleasant or compassionate diary
For any alien to behold.

Peter Vealey

Amy (all I wanted was you to be human).

Hollywood dreams are back on screen.
Night after night.
Only the foolish can believe.
Amy (all I wanted was you to be friendly.)
Filling in the gaps, girls looking at foreign snaps.
The unseen desire for a different world,
Than you really inhabit.
"I`m talking to old friends,
I haven`t seen in ten years"
Is a long time.
And you have never known me,
Or me you.
Hollywood dreams are back on the screen.
The best things remain
On celluloid forever, to be seen once only.
The woman asleep after.......
The man awake thoughtful.
The power quo must remain.

Arteries

Arteries from road to road.
Cable men, latter day saints?
Bringing the sky man`s wobbly heaven.
Arteries.
Where once there was communication
Now there`s only underground propaganda.
On the news, in the papers.
Arteries.
A modern community nightmare.
And no-one consulted,
In the vacuum of the junk mail
Bin routine.
Arteries joining up all over
An urban landscape.
Sirens wail.
Endless planes
Thunder rumble.
But no-one hears the coming judgement
Of new age politicking!

Blonde Bimboesque

Blonde bimboesque.
Vital forward teetering,
To a world
You can never inhabit.
Be seen to be going
Somewhere, anywhere?
Blonde bimboesque.
Daughters and Mothers in tow.
Who`s more sad, more mad?
To remove any wobbly fairy
Who might stop?
Their pride and joy,
From on high.
Blonde bimboesque,
Where are you?
Afternoons in paradise.
The shot was clinical and cheap.
But we had to do it for the
Heat it provides.
Blonde bimboesque,
Vital forward stumbling
To a world.
Mere you and I,
Just voyeurs inadequate.
Their age of fifteen-minute fame
Was over,
While you were only
Watching and washing up.

Box of dreams

Looking in a box of dreams.
I saw you looking in a box.
One night, one day
We'll be far away.
Still searching though
For a box of dreams.

Peter Vealey

Cacti Corner

Thinking of all the people,

I've been through.

In time.

Like a party.

They were never here.

Just for the celebration of the fear.

It's clear.

You can make it

If you steer

Wide of cacti corner.

Which toast did they leave after?

What boast was too much for

Their indigestion?

Laughing till their heart gave way.

Is it better to be seen

Dead than alive?

Drinking about people,

Loving people at cacti corner.

That's honestly all we do!

Particular

A little film of protection,

From your sneering, jeering protection.

All our aim is someone to

Survive outside cacti corner.

Capitalism Blues

I am over the worst,

I've fallen far from the thirst.

The need to be seen.

Sometimes I even dare to dream

Of one day never recycling,

Being just another mere foot soldier.

Of that bad, sad old dream.

"Commuterville"

All we have got is self-important

Nobodies.

Keeping in contact at all times.

Going to see "tribute bands".

Nothing is real.

Only an illusion of respectability.

All we have really got is

Mobile phone mania.

Status is all.

Meaning of life-bah!

That's for a bored rainy day,

They secretly pray, will never come.

Conversations

Interminable lost time
In waiting rooms.
Conversations no one
Remembers.
Evolving life?
A pattern of disrepute.
Middle-class girls
With well-heeled, casual clothes.
Dream of concern,
And of working for more
Than yuppie values.
That designers and marketing people
Invariably have.
I sleep the dozy ill inducing
Sleep of the train.
That everyone does.
Amidst the darkness
Of a winter weekend,
Fades into another day of irresponsible damage.
That safe closeted "Times" readers.
Will never comprehend
As long as
The "Thunderer" is published,
Britannia will rule
Forever.

Cooked Politics

Multiply the misery,

Subtract the situation.

Divide and destroy and

Add the alternative equation endlessly!

"Couples"

Couples are often couples.
Couples are couples and singles.
Couples are rarely one.
Couples are just couples,
Trying to be the one and all-time together.
Couples are two.
Love is the one feeling of two.
Couples are glad,
Couples are sad.
Couples are mad about one another,
Not always the other.
Couples are life!
Without the loving,
There are no couples.
Couples are alone,
Likened to stone.
When the days
Are no more
Of being a "Couple!"

"Different Perspectives."

"Old Harold won four out of five

In ten years.

They've had three in thirteen

The other lot

But then again it is Labour!"

"They`re bloody idealists,

Aren't they?

That crowd!"

Empire state of mind

Heard some old guys say,
"What we need today is a
Coalition of
Non-party politicians.
Not all this old hat.
Class war of attrition.
This country has gone to pot.
And I too hate this lot!"
What we need, is a
Role to play.
As we rewrite the real history.
Of yesterday.
Get out the sabre knives
Of tears.
And let`s get back
That knighthood zeal.

Eternity's moment with me

Slunk in a car.
The drivers` gone for a star.
Evensong, I am left with your delicate ballad.
Play it like a forlorn salad.
The tune is swept and sung.
In the moon`s lonely fun.
Slunk in a car.
The drivers` gone for a star.
Evensong I am left with your delicate ballad.
I`ve had too much traffic salad.
The tune is sweet and sour.
In the moons lonely fun.
The apathetic trees.
Are lucky enough
To have both
Beauty and disease.
In my tortured mind.
I`m torn and blind.
Stretched across the tranquil mime.
Thrown and mocked by my own worldliness.
Eternity has deserted us
Just as we deserted eternity,
For an existence of mistaken fraternity.
All we can do
Is juggle and gamble
In the traffic salad.
I`ll send my soul,
Soiled and low.
A few inadequate words
To blow like bubbles.
Quick and fleeting
In to the vast night.
The drivers' gone for a star
Soon again we are eating
That familiar monotonous traffic salad.

Peter Vealey

From our frailties within

From our frailties within.
To the streets of dirty, dusty Dublin.
Of Shaw, Wilde, Yeats, Joyce and all.
How they fought so desperately
For the righted "wrong".
Our consciences are shredded
Torn and shallow,
Bereft of
Empire cloak and skin.
I walked these roads of
Republicanism.
Meetings still held of
Fragile socialism.
Something my country
Will never breathe in.
Sadly I feel more akin
To Irish roots of brethren.

Holiday Dublin 2009

Greed

If you set greed free,
It does not mean necessarily,
That greed will set you free.

G20 (Level Playing Field?)

At the G20 "Beano",

They are pontificating on

Rich food, thirsty limos and the

Unknown dangers of the long-term unemployed.

Video chess dramas,

Of passing pieces of

Varying importance and competence.

The level playing field.

With you, as the evergreen pawn.

The sleight on breakfast television.

About no-one holding their breath.

Is to be overturned at a later commission.

(No-one can be seen to out-establish the establishment!)

"I`m all right jackism".

I gave blood.
I wanted to feel good
About myself.
It hurt.
I never returned.
I cared so much for humanity.
Desperately, somehow needed to
Share.
In today`s ever present
I`m all right jackism.
I bared my soul in counselling.
For the search to be `human`,
And be among all of you.
But belatedly realised.
Like words and pictures.
We can travel everywhere anew,
And still be lost in time.
Amongst the dogged images,
They refused to let die.
I tried to communicate
On the doorstep, in my car.
The way it should be.
But what did I receive?
A form saying-
It doesn`t pay,
And it`s time for us all to
Go back to
"I`M ALL RIGHT, JOHN BULL JACKISM"!

If peace was an army?

If peace was an army?

They would have fired the General long ago.

If peace was a football team,

The Manager,

Would have been signing on the "dole".

If peace was such a long cherished dream.

Why do we always

Fall back to conflict?

If peace ever resembled the human spirit.

Then these sad clowns

We put up as gods.

Would have been relegated to

The backwoods of humanity,

Early in their careers.

If peace was an advertising agency,

The company would have been in receivership.

With the dictating directors squealing,

We couldn't get

The product across to Joe Punter!

If peace was an army,

Then the peace wouldn't be worth having.

Immortal

We all feel we are
Immortal as
Money flashing down the drain.
Where`s the pain?
Time waits for no one.
So it goes to the (end of the show)
We all feel this place is
Unbreakable, the tender look.
All took for granted.
Inevitably as rain follows shine.
Isn`t love always mine.
Never (ever) yet blind.
Young as delusions go.
The time of your power
Weeps slow.
Gracious as the night
Letting go.
Tomorrow is an innocent,
Yet to know life.

Peter Vealey

Inferences

Inferences are drawn
By the slow drip of bias and prejudice.
Inferences are believed,
Eventually.
If a lie is told long enough.
It becomes the new reality.
However daft.
Always give me
Someone who believes from the gut.
Rather that,
Than the hackneyed cliché.
The unhappy home truths of the
Cynical "floating voter".
Inferences are drawn,
And fashion is created
Often by default.
The individual's needs are promoted
Ahead of the collective.
Yet we are all wounded
By the selfish and narrow of mind.
Inferences are collected
Like bad laws.
Changed too readily by hunger-driven
Riotous disorder.
And always, always distorted
By an end-of-pier
Hall of mirrors perspective.

Knitwork

Is this what it all
Comes down to?
At the tired pith of days.
Drunken anaesthesia and pledges.
Never the reality in
Cold day of morn.
Warm smoky dreams
That evaporate
On tomorrows' vicious hearts.
That in the end,
For all common humanity
Mean nothing.
But the knitwork of locality cliques,
And familiarity of winking
Misunderstanding.
Rural harshness is there for all
To see,
When it comes down to
Family interests.

Land of the Ghouls

Well I have been in pubs,
Where they have been eating
Coleslaw and cold sausages.
I've drunk Carling black labels
With the polished phonies.
I've been at Bishopsgate, the City
And St.Paul's.
But no more that's,
The Land of the Ghouls.

Limited Consciences

In the land of the limited conscience,

Thoughtlessness is King.

Natureforce

The canopy is moving.
Free will or not.
The puffy, complacent
Grey and white clouds,
Signal an ominous dawn.
The canopy is moving.
All the fresh change of yesterday.
Changes anew again.
To unseen, unknown worlds
Of light and tragedy.
The canopy is moving,
Restless and fickle
Into night and day.
Where fortune is stemmed,
Then ebbs away.
The canopy is moving,
Reckless at heart.
Wistful, wild and
Untamed of spirit.
All your new hopes and dreams,
Are no sedative
On its life-force
Now or ever.

Neighbours

Neighbours should be more
Than a half-hidden hello.
Humanity should be more
Than an old-fashioned ideal.
Neighbours, it starts and ends here
To confide, to befriend?
A few casual words that can
Breed tolerance and understanding.
It starts and ends here,
Within the heart and soul of everyone.
So why are the lights
 Always on red?

Newspeak

Looking for the good news story.

Editor strongly hints,

It's imperative we

Include something with the "aah"feel!

Coerce you, compromise me.

Patronise the victims.

Trivialise the controversy.

Always looking out

For the good news story.

Christmas is so near!

Future scenarios, so full of fear.

Keep the Bogeyman near!

All we need to do is keep grinding

Everyone's hopes down.

While looking right and strong.

"On Committee."

I was self important once.
On every committee you could name!
A fancy metal rimmed folder.
Orderly black Filo-Fax,
With pens galore.
"Big fish" contacts by the score.
I shouted the odds.
From pillar to chamber.
Stamped on tables!
I liked hearing my voice,
Resonate down halls and corridors.
Without a squeak of dissent.
Onlookers turned their heads,
When I sorted them all out!
But when I died,
No one came to
Thank me.

Outstripping

Want to live
Pillar to pole.
Ice to soul.
Ragged to roll.
Want to be
Sometimes, someone
The next a non-entity.
Want to live
For chewing the scroll.
Outliving the role,
Not facing the "dole".

Over the rainbow

I remember the Lone Ranger,
Roy Rogers and all that Jazz.
Ain't got nothing on me.
Going down that horsey hill.
To the stirring sounds of old Will Tell.
Dust everywhere.
9/11,
Heroes everywhere.
"Wild-West dreaming".
John Wayne on sick leave.
I remember
Leonard Slye,
Trying to put "right"
Where "wrong" had
Pervaded the sheer
Azure skies
Of Arizona.
Or somewhere
Over the rainbow
Way-out West (of Hollywood).

Paper Tigers

You can never
Have the last word.
Whatever you say.
It doesn't matter,
They will outlast you
In the trivia stakes.
Nothing is sacred.
Words are empty, but words are all
A famous playwright might
Have said.
You can never be more than they.
The doctrine is self-righteous
And pious.
On Armageddon day,
They'll tell you
It was your fault,
Not theirs.
That it came down
To this.

Passing Hero

A once youthful figure aged by,
The responsibilities of unrealistic
Panegyric expectations.
Now a forlorn, chastened, Methuselah figure
Of disheartenment.
Held to unremitting ransom and bias,
Answerable to none but themselves.
As beacons of democracy and sublime wisdom.
Amidst the constant drizzle of a disappointing
summer.
Uttering olive-branch words
Of hindsight perspective.
To you ever trusting Joe Public.
Our lives must go on.
Albeit on panic control.
Petrol, the latest cause
Of the so-called
Downtrodden masses.
The scapegoat, procrastinating politicians.
Remote in yearly ritualising
By the bay.
Portrayed unerringly,
As masters and harbingers
Of betrayal and disillusionment.

Perfect age of mind

When is your perfect age of mind?
When your core of days is as
Ripe as a sun-kissed apple.
Looking back is filled with pitfalls.
Back then or there,
There were confrontations of control and ego,
Amongst idyllic settings.
Photos of splendid happiness!
Bad haircut days though amidst
The look-alike paradise.
When was your perfect age of mind?
When your core of days was as
Ripe as a sun-kissed apple.
A date, an hour
A passing moment.
You could never hold on to
Secure.
Like sand slipping through
Hands, gripping too late.
In a perfect age of mind.
The quest is over,
Long live the King of Fools!

Persona

The landscape was as always,
Changing but unchanging.
The insight less dynamic
By age.
The fanciful dreams worn down by
Various, unkind impatient words.
The smile
Thinner than before.
Persona of a fading optimist.
The dawning winter,
Approaching of his life.
Unshakeable loyalty, tested
By the current harsh
All-consuming fad of me, myself and I
Fashioned by counselling centres.
And books, read so sparsely even by
So-called experts.
With Vacant-Attention-Syndrome.
The landscape closed in
On another night.
Tight-lipped,
Almost taunting
On his weariness.
At a struggling belief,
Called-
The first day of
The rest of your life.

Peter Vealey

Picture Postcard

Picture postcard.
I could send
You one of
Where I am
But cards
Are only cards
Like hearts,
Can't change
Hearts.
Tractors far away,
Farmer's labourer
Working in the
Damp chill.
But never really
With a reluctant will.
Sheep ramble munching
Constantly.
Following, mooching
Timelessly.
Birds peck berries
Incessantly.
Flying alert,
Tree to tree.
Before the harsh
Farmer's gun,
Upsets, but only
Momentarily, the tranquillity.
Strange to a town lad,
Who gropes to understand?
A thousand different lives
Within a land.
But tied to convention,
I'll send you a
Picture postcard
And try to relate,
Meaninglessly,
What we did
On such and such a date.

"Play Misty"

Watching yet another re-run
"Play Misty for me".
Where the jazzy sixties muzak
Runs along the coastal dusk.
No-one can save the innocent detective.
From becoming a victim.
The gallant Joe dies dumb.
Still, all is put to right.
The speedy macho machine will
Never run dry.
Along the sea roads
Good must survive.
The seedy die brutally.
Old Clint has his doubts and demons.
But in the end
America and God survive
Intact and indivisible.

Politicians` song

Pose, pose wherever you may be.
This is the land of the pose you see.
Pose, pose in public and on "telly".
Make a statement, oh so urgently.
Then put it under an exhaustive enquiry.
And forget it permanently.
Pose, pose wherever you may be.
Politicians` and Police are exempt you see.
Pose, pose wherever you may be
I never quite said that.
Whatever you claim.
Pose, pose in public.
Talk and smile brightly.
Take nothing seriously.
In a day or three.
I'll double-talk and deny and
Oh you'll never frame me.
This is the land of the pose you see.
Pose, pose wherever you may be,
If we catch too many.
They'll be riots you'll see!
I'd rather we let a few thugs go
Than have complaints you know.
So don't blame me.
This is the land of the pose you see!

Poverty

People laugh and bustle past

"Naff" cardboard city buskers and beggars.

Amidst winter's icy blast.

But poverty and homelessness

Are no laughing matter!

Quangoitis

September,
Panting up a hill.
Rain coming down hard
Eye-level contact
With a "brolly".
Are you in there or avoiding?
The young nouveau rich
Playing at men by numbers.
In suits they've yet to fill.
Are splashing clumsily downstream.
While the world appeal merchants
Are considered naive innocents abroad.
In the streets of your homes.
Lepers in disguise.
Who knows where it ends?
The obsession with unelected dream fakirs.
Taking the pain away from you.
Where the quack used to pretend to care.
"What can you expect
In this day and age?"

Saplings

Saw these saplings

At a funeral.

Flashy, restless and rustling.

Bling on heat!

Dying to show,

(Those in the know).

Amidst carnage and regret.

Their new zeal of life.

Saw these saplings in black.

Fresh as war paint.

On the old trusted values

Of displacement,

And confused disheartenment.

Sleeping in a sane hell

Do you decay?

In the houses you stay.

Do they, do you, do they?

You relax so well!

Sleeping in a sane hell.

Walls keep you prisoner

In a subtle sort of way.

The disease spreads fast.

Ooh and it lasts!

Do you decay, do you, do they?

Sleeping in a sane hell.

You manage everything quite well

Considering,

You are existing in a sane hell.

In the houses you stay.

Do you decay?

Eventually, do you, do they?

Stigma

My toe nails are growing long.
I must be more at ease.
So I tell myself
Anxiously.
Looking for signs of acceptance.
A vain and valueless hunt.
Best ignored like your frown.
My inner voice screams
"Be yourself!"
Though softer, less assertive
Than in days of youthful bravado.
Stigma!
As ever the knocking shop
Of hate.
"You're different!"
Yet aren`t we all and individual,
From day one on earth
To our last breath!

Tea and Rock cake mornings

Tea and rock cake mornings.

Dry skin blues.

Bloodshot eyes from paper strained times.

Black creased, greasy trousers.

Petrol fumes and harsh engines

Screaming through the day.

Blackening the world grey.

Dusty streets and dowdy sandwich bars.

Red coughing buses.

Frightening screaming tubes

Tearing at my soul.

Oh the heavy city!

When will the sun

Shine on you?

Pin-striped broad walks,

Immaculate ties

And staring "hawks".

Tender Trees

Tender trees I saw in
Harsh fields of men.
Where respectability
Bites and never ends.
Tied to a cottage world.
Of knowing who is your friend.
Tender young trees, I saw in
Harsh fields of men.
Parish meetings of
"Character" chairmen,
That never bend,
And always blame
It on the "government".
Tender trees, I saw amongst
Harsh fields of men.

Peter Vealey

The Framework

Watching the "Starsky and Hutch" re-runs.
Too tired to change the score.
Listening to the local pubs
Inevitable bore.
"I don`t do factory jobs anymore"
(I guess I never did).
The sun is out in my sunny,
Small village world.
Egos run amok in
Claustrophobic rooms of no power.
The humour of mediocrity.
Always to hide from
The inevitable conclusion.
That we all live and die,
And that life is more, much more
Than mere people.

The laughter of desperation

I know that laughter so

Well.

Of the "what the hell?"

Brigade.

The "we are all going to die anyway" mentality.

"What's the good of caring.

Being a do-gooder.

It don't make money,

And I don't need the stress,

No way!

My life has been far from cosy".

Oh I could encapsulate

That laughter so well.

It's like a skeletal

Death rattle.

The laughter of dinosaurs.

Desperate, beached and selfish.

I've stood near there,

And it's no place to stay.

The refuge's empty.

The light, dims a little more

For all of us,

When their howl is heard.

The Power behind the Throne

The charities are out in force.

It's Saturday.

Conscience on a stick.

Anything is possible,

Except for revolution

In the U.K.

The P.M. at Chequers.

Fund raising no doubt.

The grey suit on a hanger.

"Val Doonican" pullovers

Back on Frost Sunday Breakfast interviews.

Two and a half year's rent

Paid for.

Peerage planned.

King Pawn!

You were never number 1.

It was always her

You know whom……..

The Seductive world of advertising

The seductive world of advertising,
Has drawn you in.
Relentless fire-proof!
They want you (more than they need you.)
The change is coming,
But it's not what they are telling you.
The seductive world of advertising,
Is like brown bread or white.
We all know what we prefer,
And my parents` doctor
Swore
White bread sent you
Mad!
And we wouldn't want that
Would we!
We are all normal aren't we?
The seductive world of advertising
Is all encompassing?
And incomplete
As starched fodder.

The Whitewashers

The whitewashers are here today.

All spick and span.

Dressed in black

To cover our sins and lack of respect.

They will have another tomorrow.

For they're never short of work

A token kind word or two

Falls on indifferent ears.

In sparsely populated churches.

People in nice suits and discreet dresses.

Telling us he wasn't so bad.

The whitewashers are here today.

To cover our pain, not his loss of aspiration.

All the plans and dreams he never "got round to".

Still we slowly arrive in patiently splendid limos,

And wait for the day

To pass away.

Thusandthem

In the land of thusandthem.

There is no great divide.

All these "local difficulties"

Have been resolved.

Thusandthem, thanusdthem

Sing out!

The war is over here.

Long live

Thusandthem!

Tinseland

Get me home quick.
The concreteness of it all,
Scares me solid.
Tinsel dreams are no dreams, no life.
Take me back
Where the darkness
Has no scar of urban light.
Beauty untouched,
By the bewildered parody
Of a plan.
Created by mere
Man.
When will my eyes smile
Again?
This world on a timetable,
Spinning sour and
Faulty.
Soon to fall.
Tinseland.
Like movie dreams,
So far, yet so close.

To fill newspapers(to sell copy)

The talk in the "silly season".

Is of crop circles

And mystery big cats.

Never quite found or properly clarified.

To fill newspapers.

In the past,

It was for collecting chips

At the seaside.

In August or December.

At the end of the day.

Their relevance

To the fabric of the nation,

Just as much.

To fill newspapers.

Blame is all.

Scapegoats to bring on,

The new King.

To delude is all.

The real answers are not their concern.

To John Lennon

They never really appreciated you.

Put you on a front page.

Blamed you a hero.

Wrote many songs

That got too close.

And though I am not the

One who will miss you most.

Your music was so underrated, misunderstood.

The love in your songs.

The hope in your caring, despairing heart.

What more could you say?

It wasn't your fault,

Just a world in decay.

Trust status?

Our schools are on constant voucher appeals.

For computers and books.

N.H.S. hospitals propped up by charities.

Overlooked by Rottweiler's in designer suits.

(Formerly of right-wing think tanks).

Chasing that elusive dream of perfection.

Courses on all kinds of motivation.

Nothing is thrown out.

Except for humility.

It's so redundant, so passé!

One Last Flower

One last flower
in the garden.

One last spluttering song of summer.

One last linger.

On another year passing.

Looking at you.

Can I brood or move on?

Rebirth or silence.

Pretty as flowers are.

They're only petals, roots and earth.

Nowhere!

When compared to the intricate puzzle that is
LOVE, HATE, BLOOD & WATER!

Unthinking

We are the main killers

Of the natural resources

Of Earth.

The internet and media briskly announced.

As if it's some great surprise.

We ravage unthinking.

We speak unthinking.

We learn unchallenging too often.

We are the main killers,

Of the natural resources

Of Mother Earth.

Nothing will change,

Nothing can change.

Till profit is God,

All knowing

No more!

In the boardroom and bedroom of mind.

Unthinking deserts us all

Remorselessly.

Voicing Fears

What am I scared of?
A few interested listeners
Miles away.
Minds on other, closer people
Familiar places.
What am I worried about?
Will you clap, or will you jeer?
A day and half in contemplation
Of the unobtainable warm cheer.
You're either in the bar animating
Or looking out of the windows.
Old conversations milked to a turn.
What am I scared of?
I'm only like you,
Aren't I?

Whistleblowers and Snitchers

Whistleblowers and snitchers

Are going online.

Trying they say to rid us of crime.

What happened to "Honest Joe Bloggs"?

And his close friend down the alley,

"Joe Public"?

They were "seen off "

I heard by,

Mary Whitehouse,

Big Brother and even

Citizen Kane joined in!

Rumoured to scowl,

"Give them a good kicking!"

Wise Owl Blues

Nothing has changed,
The distances remain the same.
Whatever we do, the differences
Came through.
Old friends and how the memory seemed
Fine.
Till we bring it into the present,
And hear the wise owl say-
"You shouldn't
Try to recapture
The waters under the bridge."
And clichés too many to a fist.
Nothing's changed.
We look older
And the sentimentality's the same.
A hug to embrace our walls,
And go off to cement
Our entrenchment.

Within Suits

How much do you lose?
Within suits.
Spend half of your evenings
Sitting stiff,
Scared of sneezing.
Scared of pleasing yourself.
Within suits!
How much do you lose?
You're wearing the right shoes.
You can't break out!
You're within suits!
How much do you lose?

Particular

Easters 1999

Peter Vealey

Smiling 2010